The Inuit
People of the North

Richard Alexander

Rosen Classroom™

New York

Published in 2014 by The Rosen Publishing Group, Inc.
29 East 21st Street, New York, NY 10010

Book Design: Mickey Harmon

Photo Credits: Cover, p. 13 Sue Flood/The Image Bank/Getty Images; pp. 3, 4, 6, 8, 10, 12, 14–16, 18, 20, 22–24 (fur) Filip Obr/Shutterstock.com; p. 5 PavelSvoboda/Shutterstock.com; p. 7 smudger/Shutterstock.com; p. 9 Luke Betts/Wikipedia.org; pp. 11, 21 (inside igloo) Wayne R Bilenduke/Stone/Getty Images; p. 15 (shoes) Kletr/Shutterstock.com; p. 15 (knife) BMJ/Shutterstock.com; p. 15 (coat) Daderot/Wikipedia.org; p. 17 Luciana Whitaker/America 24-7/Getty Images; p. 19 PHB.cz (Richard Semik)/Shutterstock.com; p. 21 (igloos) Rita Januskeviciute/Shutterstock.com; p. 22 (family) Konstantin Shervtsov/Shutterstock.com.

ISBN: 978-1-4777-2548-1
6-pack ISBN: 978-1-4777-2549-8

Manufactured in the United States of America

CPSIA Compliance Information: Batch #CS13RC: For further information contact Rosen Publishing, New York, New York at 1-800-237-9932.

Contents

Who Are the Inuit?

What would it be like to live in the Arctic? That part of the world is quiet, cold, and covered in snow. In winter, **temperatures** go far below zero. Even in summer, some parts are covered in snow and ice. Some people have lived in the Arctic for many years. They're the Inuit.

The Inuit live in northern parts of the United States, Canada, Greenland, and Russia. In the United States and Canada, the name is used for several Native American groups. Their way of life has helped them survive in one of our world's coldest **environments**.

"Inuit" refers to the group of people, while "Inuk" refers to one person.

The Inuit are very special. The name applies to several societies, but they're grouped together because they live in the same area and have similar ways of life. However, each society is special in its own way. The societies have different beliefs and even speak different languages.

People believe the Inuit first lived in Asia. They may have crossed a land bridge into North America thousands of years ago. They have lived in the North ever since.

What do you think the Inuit must do to survive in these parts of the world?

1
2
3
4
KEY
- where the Inuit live
1 - United States (Alaska)
2 - Canada
3 - Greenland
4 - Russia

Speaking Inuktitut

Many Inuit people speak a language called Inuktitut. However, the way one group of Inuit speaks may sound completely different from the way another group speaks. Inuktitut can also be written in many different ways. It changes based on where the Inuit live.

The Inuit speak other languages, too, depending on where they live. Inuit kids in the United States and Canada learn English and French in school. In Greenland, they learn Danish and English. Inuit kids in Russia may learn Russian and English.

"Inuit" means "the people" in Inuktitut.

Nunavut in the North

Many Inuit people live in an area of Canada called Nunavut. The Inuit people have lived there for many years, but Nunavut didn't become an official territory until 1999. Its government makes rules and laws to protect the Inuit people.

Nunavut is one place that shows how life among the Inuit has changed. While the people who live there are modern, they still respect and practice **traditional** customs. They do this because their way of life has helped them survive for thousands of years in cold environments.

The Inuit have lived in the area now known as Nunavut for over 4,000 years.

The Inuit and Animals

Before grocery stores, the Inuit could only eat the food in their environment. It was too cold and icy to grow plants, so they fished and hunted instead.

The Inuit hunted both on land and in the water. On land, they hunted caribou, polar bears, and sometimes foxes. In the water, they hunted seals and whales. The Inuit got a lot of fat and protein from eating so much meat. Fat and protein can be made into energy, which helped the Inuit stay warm and grow strong.

Hunters used harpoons to hunt whales. Harpoons are long and have a pointy end. Inuit harpoons were made of animal bones.

The Inuit people have always had a deep respect for animals. Like other Native American groups, the Inuit depended on animals for survival. Animals weren't just used for food, though. The Inuit used every part of an animal, including skin, bones, and fur.

Animal skins were used to make tents and boats. Bones were used to make sharp tools such as knives and harpoons. Fur was used as clothing, which kept the Inuit warm in such cold temperatures.

The Inuit needed animals for more than just food. They used them in every area of their lives.

Skins, Bones, and Fur

animal skin	bones	fur
covering of boats	frames of boats	clothing
tents	knives	gloves
shoes	tools	blankets

In Water and on Land

The Inuit used different kinds of boats. Hunters used small, narrow boats called qajaqs (GAH-yahgz). These were made of sealskin and only carried one person. The best part of the qajaq was that the passenger could easily right it if it flipped over. This is where the word "kayak" comes from.

Another boat was the umiaq (OO-mee-ag). That means "woman's boat" in Inuktitut. It was longer and wider. The Inuit used it to carry many people at once, plus supplies and even their dogs!

Women and men had different jobs in Inuit communities. Can you tell what those jobs were based on their boats?

You may think of dogs as pets, but they did important jobs for the Inuit. Teams of dogs pulled sleds over snow and ice. Hunters rode on the sleds with their supplies. The sled dogs could go farther and faster in one day than an Inuk hunter could on foot.

These special dogs did much more than just pull sleds. They used their great sense of smell to hunt seals. They also kept Inuit villages safe. These dogs are still around today!

Sled dogs have big, furry coats to keep them warm in cold environments. Huskies and Alaskan Malamutes are both sled dogs.

On the Move

The Inuit were always on the move, so they didn't live in houses like they do today. Their homes had to be moved easily or created on the spot from **materials** in their environment—including snow and ice!

The Inuit used bricks of ice and snow to make igloos. Though they were made of snow, the inside of igloos was warm. It kept hunters out of the wind and cold. Some Inuit still use igloos today during hunting trips.

Igloos are dome shaped. The shape was important, since the Inuit didn't need to build inside walls to hold up the roof.

Past and Present

The Inuit were able to survive in the North because they learned how to **adapt** to their environment. Their hunting methods, tools, and homes were perfect for their cold surroundings.

The Inuit are a very special group of people. Their lives are modern now, but they still use practices from long ago. Keeping these traditions alive is one way to honor their past. Would you like to live in the Arctic like the Inuit?

Glossary

adapt (uh-DAPT) To change to fit conditions.

environment (ihn-VY-ruhn-muhnt) Everything in the world that surrounds a living thing.

material (muh-TIHR-ee-uhl) The matter used to make something.

temperature (TEHM-puhr-chur) How hot or cold something is.

traditional (truh-DIH-shuh-nuhl) Having to do with ways of life in the past.

Index